W9-CBI-744

WORKBOOKS

K Geography

Author Mark Shulman
Educational Consultant Kara Pranikoff

DK | Penguin Random House

Editors Jolyon Goddard,
Cecile Landau, Rohini Deb,
Nancy Ellwood, Margaret Parrish
Art Editor Tanvi Nathyal
Assistant Art Editor Kanika Kalra
Managing Editor Soma B. Chowdhury
Managing Art Editors Richard Czapnik,
Ahlawat Gunjan
Producer, Pre-Production Ben Marcus
Producer Christine Ni
DTP Designer Anita Yadav

First American Edition, 2015
Published in the United States by DK Publishing
345 Hudson Street, New York, New York 10014

Copyright © 2015 Dorling Kindersley Limited
A Penguin Random House Company
10 9 8 7 6 5
005–271014–Mar/2015

All rights reserved.
Without limiting the rights under copyright reserved above,
no part of this publication may be reproduced, stored in or
introduced into a retrieval system, or transmitted, in any form,
or by any means (electronic, mechanical, photocopying,
recording, or otherwise), without the prior written
permission of the copyright owner.
Published in Great Britain by Dorling Kindersley Limited.

A catalog record for this book
is available from the Library of Congress.
ISBN: 978-1-4654-2850-9

DK books are available at special discounts when purchased
in bulk for sales promotions, premiums, fund-raising, or
educational use. For details, contact: DK Publishing Special
Markets, 345 Hudson Street, New York, New York 10014
SpecialSales@dk.com

Printed and bound in Hong Kong

All images © Dorling Kindersley Limited
For further information see: www.dkimages.com

A WORLD OF IDEAS
SEE ALL THERE IS TO KNOW

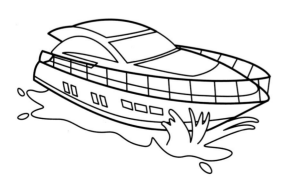

Contents

This chart lists all the topics in the
book. Once you have completed
each page, stick a star in the
correct box below.

FACTS

Geography is about the world around you. The people who study geography are called geographers. Geographers study nature. They study things such as the mountains, rivers, and forests. Geographers also study the way humans use and change nature when they make things like cities, parks, and bridges.

Circle the things that a geographer might study.

mountain

city

butterfly

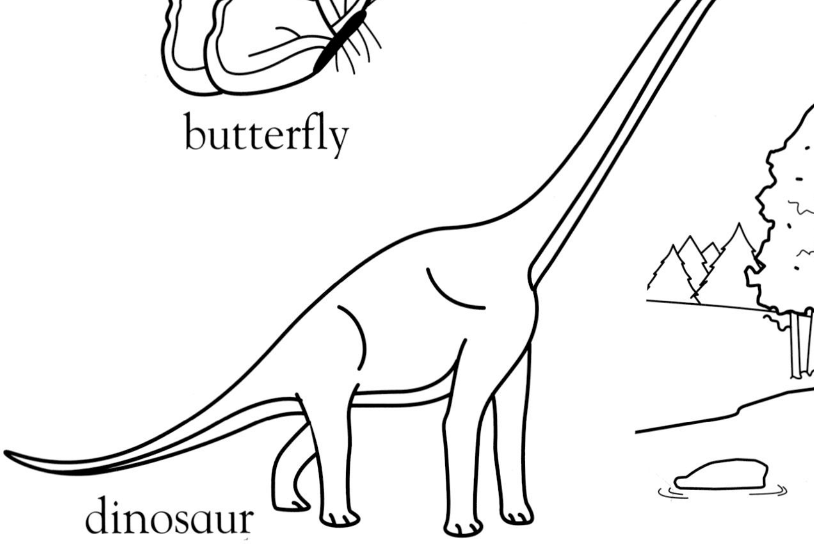

dinosaur

river

You live on a planet called Earth. Earth is one of eight planets in our solar system. All the planets in a solar system share the same sun. Earth travels around the sun once every year. When your part of Earth is tilted toward the sun, it is summer. When your part of Earth is tilted away from the sun, it is winter.

Here is a picture of our solar system.
Earth is the third planet from the sun.
Circle the planet Earth.

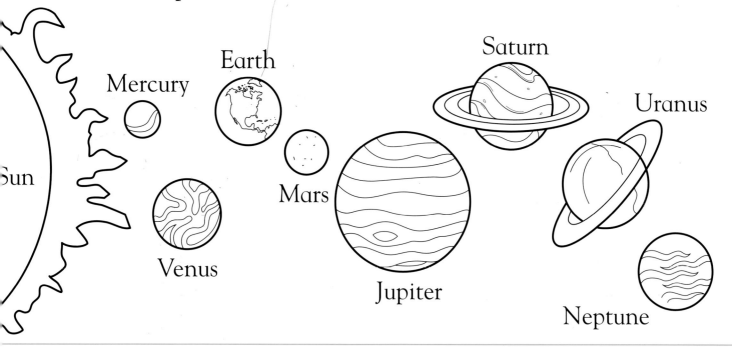

Put a check (✔) for the correct answer.

When is Earth tilted toward the sun? winter ☐ summer ✔

What does Earth travel around once every year? sun ✔   moon ☐

FACTS

A globe is a map of planet Earth. It is shaped like a ball, just like planet Earth. A globe shows all the land and water on Earth. Most globes are small enough for a person to hold.

Look at the globe below, and then read the list at the side of it. Circle the things in the list that you can find on the globe.

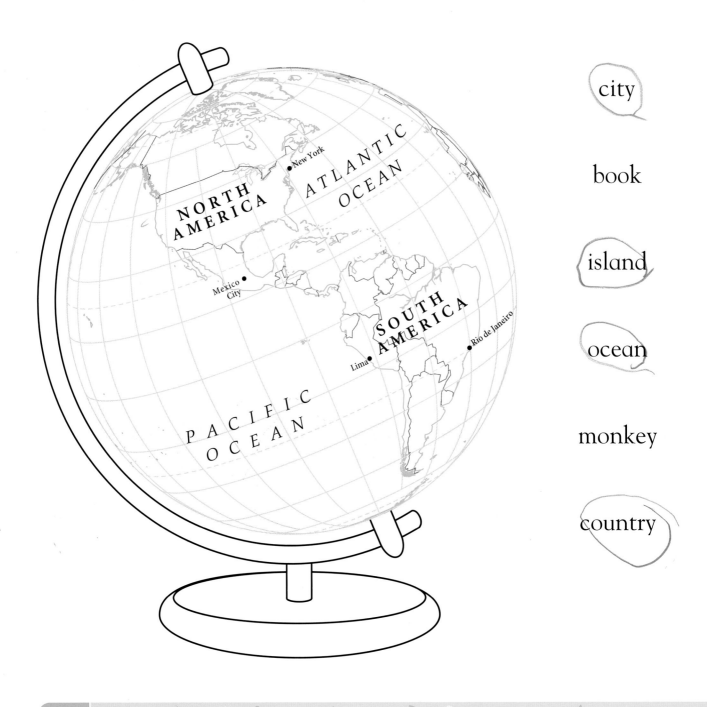

city

book

island

ocean

monkey

country

There are many different kinds of maps. A globe is shaped like a ball. Other maps are flat. They may be printed on paper, as charts, or in books. You can also see maps on the screens of computers, tablets, or phones. Flat maps can show the whole Earth or a part of it in a lot of detail.

Look at the different kinds of maps below. Write a **P** in the box under a map if the map is on paper. Write an **S** if the map is on a screen. Write a **G** if the map is a globe.

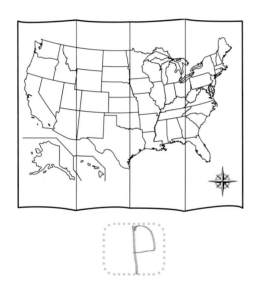

P

G

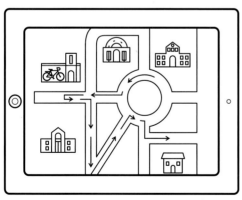

S

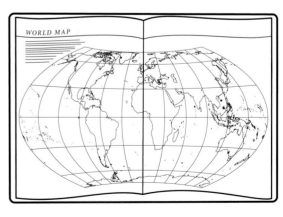

P

Different maps are used to show and explain different kinds of places. A park map shows you what is in a park. A street map shows you the streets you can travel along. A map of a room shows you the things in that room.

Below are pictures of three different places: a city, a park, and a bedroom. Draw a line to connect each place with its map.

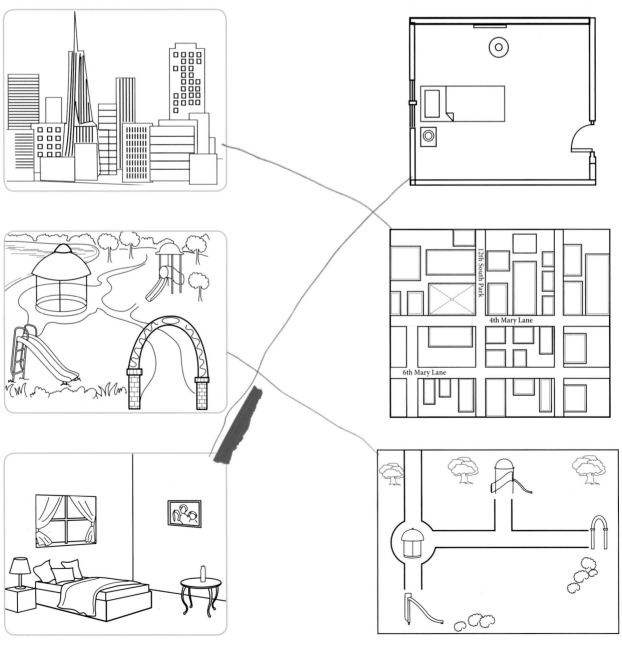

People use different maps for different reasons. A person driving a car may use a street map. Hikers may need a park map. Students and teachers may need a map of their school. There are many other kinds of maps as well.

Look at the different types of maps below. Who would use each kind of map? Draw a line to connect each map with the people who may need it.

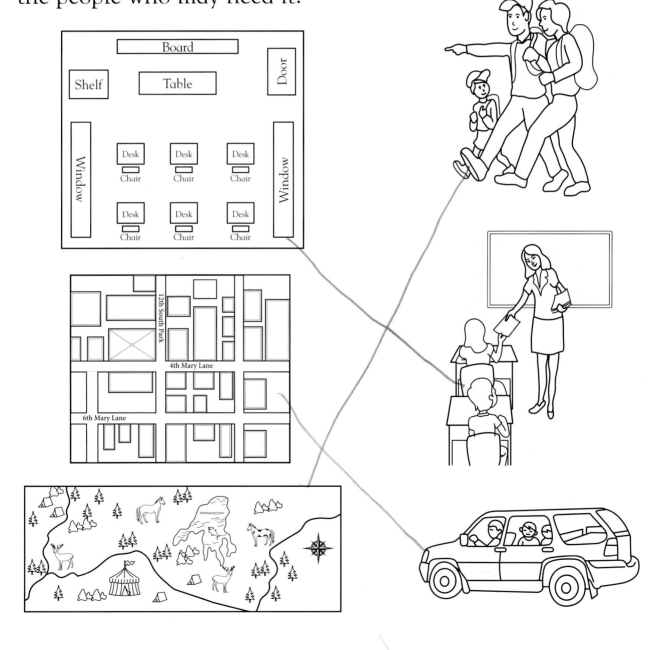

FACTS

There are four directions that you need to know about to be able to read a map. Those directions are "north," "south," "east," and "west." No matter where you are, these directions can help you reach the place that you want to go to.

Look at the globe of Earth below.
Then place your finger in the middle of Earth.
Move your finger north, up to the **N**.
Now, move your finger south, down to the **S**.

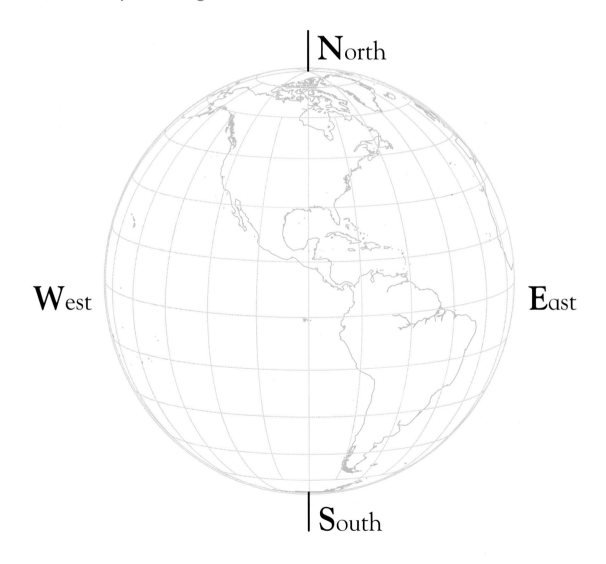

FACTS

Most maps have a tool called a compass rose. It lets you know which direction the top of the map is pointing toward. Most maps have north at the top and south at the bottom. On such maps, west is on the left and east is on the right.

This is the compass rose you will see on a map.
Color the compass rose. Trace in the letters **N**, **S**, **E**, and **W**.

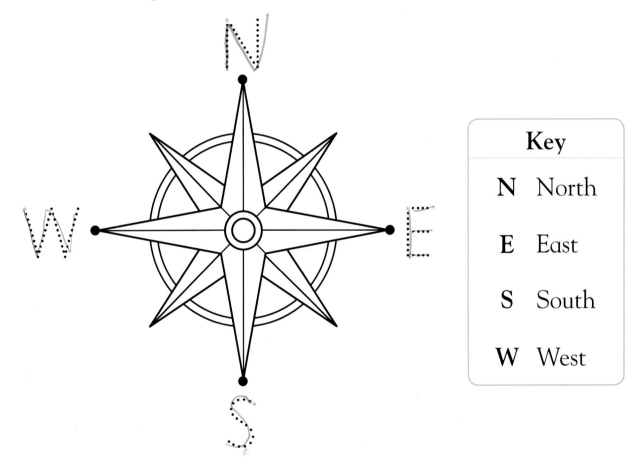

Key

N	North
E	East
S	South
W	West

Complete the four sentences below.

N is for   North .   **E** is for   East .

S is for   South .   **W** is for   west .

The direction "north" is usually found at the top of a map. When you are going north, you are moving toward the top of Earth. You may know about the frozen North Pole. That is where you will end up if you keep going north!

Find the word "north" on the compass rose, and then circle it.

Now, look at the map of an amusement park below. Imagine you are standing at the X (✗). Which two rides are to the north of you? Circle them on the map.

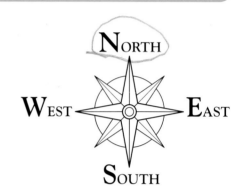

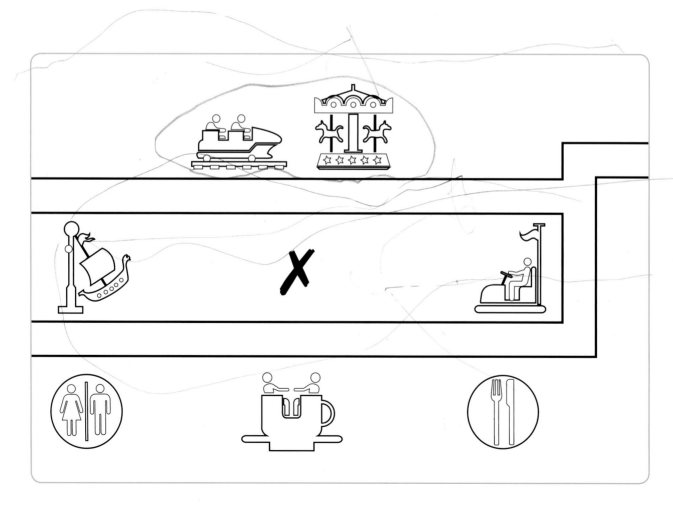

FACTS

The direction "south" is usually found at the bottom of a map. When you are going south, you are moving toward the bottom of Earth. Have you heard about the freezing South Pole? That is where you will find yourself if you keep going south!

Find the word "south" on the compass rose, and then circle it. Now look at the map of North America. Find the country of Canada. Then color the country directly south of Canada.

The direction "east" is usually found at the right side of a map. When you are going east, you are moving sideways across Earth from left to right. Did you know that the sun rises in the east?

Look at the town map below. Imagine you are standing at the X (✗). Which two buildings are to the east of you? Circle them on the map.

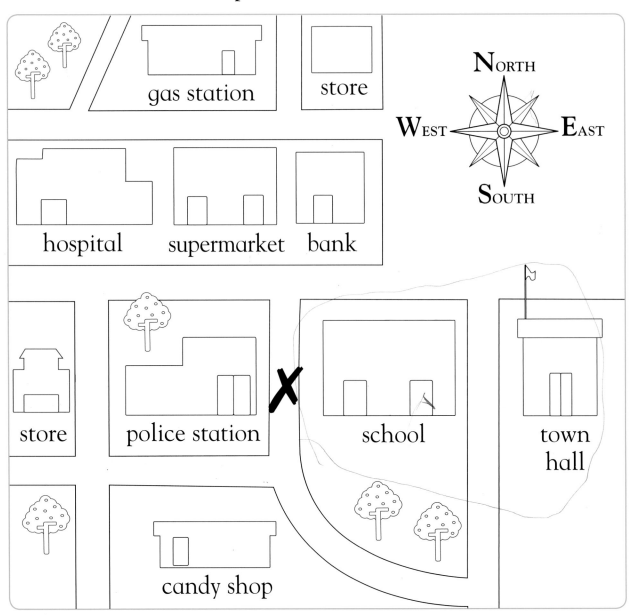

The direction "west" is usually at the left side of a map. When you are going west, you are moving across Earth from right to left. The sun sets in the west. If you can see the sun setting, you are facing west, and it is time for bed!

Look at the map of Australia below. It shows where some animals are found. Imagine you are standing at the X (✗). Circle the animal that can be found to the west of you.

FACTS

In geography, you study both the natural world and the human world. Think about a road on a mountain. The mountain is part of the natural world. It was part of our world long before there was a road. The road is part of the human world. People built the road. Geography is about understanding both the natural and the human world, and how they work together.

Use the words "natural" and "human" to complete the sentences below.

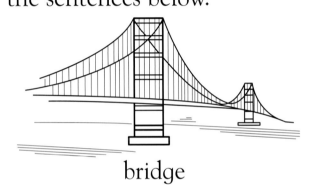
bridge

river

A river is part of the ...natural... world.

A bridge is part of the ...human... world.

Circle the picture that shows the natural world.
Put an X on the picture that shows the human world.

airport

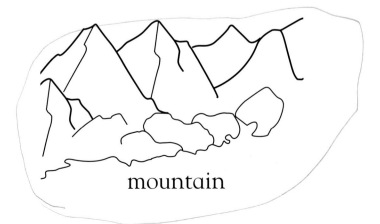
mountain

Your World ★

Your world has things from the natural world and things from the human world. The flowers and trees in a park are part of the natural world. The house you live in and your school are part of the human world.

Look around you. Draw something that is part of the natural world. Then draw something that is part of the human world.

Natural World / God made

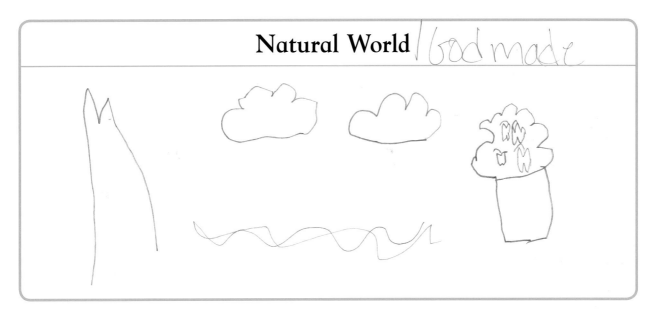

Human World / People made

17

Maps of the natural world can help people understand it better. These maps can show mountains, rivers, lakes, types of trees, and even the weather. This information can help people plan a trip as well as pack the right clothes and equipment for it.

Draw lines connecting each natural place with its map.

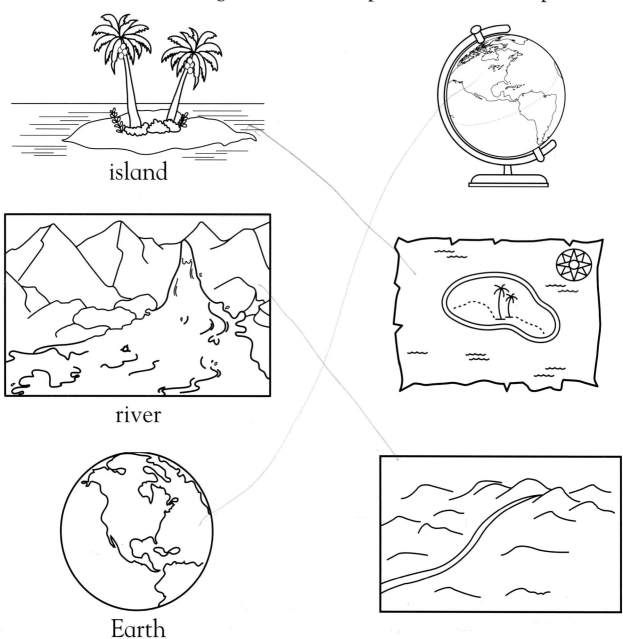

island

river

Earth

There are seven very large areas of land on Earth. These huge areas are called continents. When you look at a globe or a flat map of Earth, you will see the seven continents. The largest continent is Asia. The smallest continent is Australia.

Look at this map of the world. It shows all seven continents. Then follow the instructions below the map.

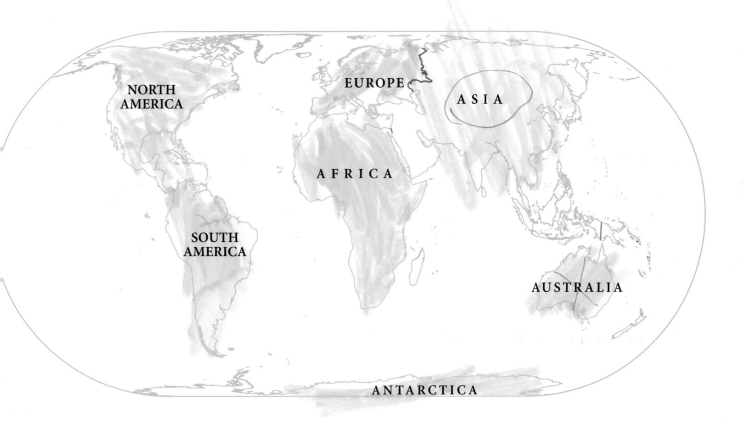

Color all the continents green.
Hint: Everything you do not color in this map is water.

Circle the name of the largest continent.
Put an X (✗) on the name of the smallest continent.

Mountains and hills are high areas of land. Hills are not as high as mountains. Some mountains are so tall that their tops reach the clouds. The tallest mountains have snow on top, even in summer.

Look at the two pictures below. Color the mountains brown. Color the hills green. Then answer the questions.

What is on top of the tallest mountain?

What is on top of the tallest hill?

Flag
goat

Forests are large areas of land that are covered with trees. There are many forests on Earth. Many different kinds of animals live inside a forest. Some are large and others are small.

Look at the picture of a forest below. There are many different kinds of animals living in this forest. Circle the animals that you can find.

The driest places on Earth are called deserts. Many are very hot in the daytime and cold at night, but some are always cold. Deserts get very little rain. Most people do not like to live in such dry places. However, a number of plants and animals have learned to live in the desert.

Look at the picture of a desert below. Circle the different kinds of animals and plants that you can find in the picture.

An island is a piece of land that is completely surrounded by water. Islands can be very large, or they can be very small.

Look at the islands of Hawaii below. Then complete the activities.

Niihau

Kauai

Oahu

Molokai

Maui

Lanai

Kahoolawe

Hawaii

Count the number of islands. How many are there?

Draw a picture of something that people may use to travel between the islands.

FACTS

An ocean is a very, very large body of water. There are five oceans on Earth, and they cover most of the planet. They are home to many different kinds of animals, such as whales, sea turtles, and fish. In fact, there are more animals in the oceans than there are on land.

Look at the map of the world below. It shows the continents surrounded by oceans. Color the oceans.

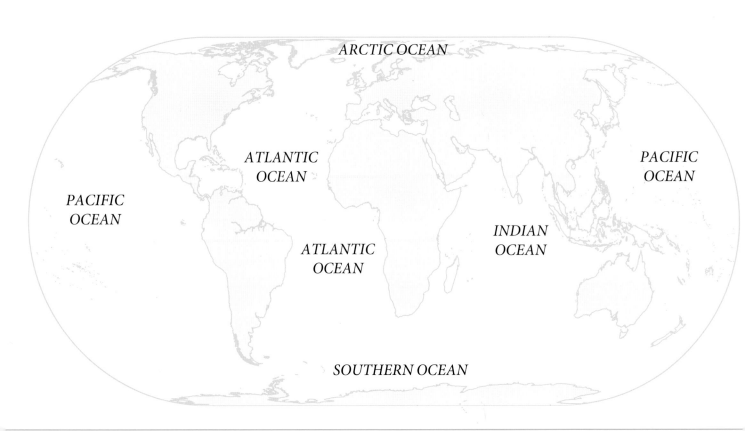

Circle the animals that live in the ocean.

whale

rabbit

seal

A lake is a large body of water surrounded by land. Some lakes are very big. People would need a large boat to go across a big lake. Other lakes are much smaller. People can cross them in a small boat.

Circle the things made by humans that you might see at a lake. Color the animals that you might also see there.

dinosaur

sailboat

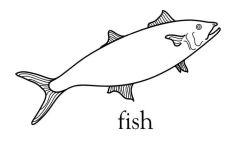

fish

baseball

life jacket

duck

FACTS

Water flows from high places to low places. A small amount of flowing water is called a stream. A large amount of flowing water is called a river. Many towns and cities are built along rivers. Rivers can be long and wide and may move very quickly. You might need a bridge or a boat to get across a river.

Circle the three things you can use to get across a river.

tractor

bridge

bicycle

motorboat

rowboat

The places humans make are part of the human world. We build roads, bridges, and tunnels to help us go places. We make cities, towns, and villages to live in. We create parks and playgrounds so we can enjoy them. All of these things can be found on a map.

Circle the pictures of things that belong to the human world.

school

beach

desert

city

zoo

A country is an area of Earth that people identify as one place.

Look at the map of the world. Then follow the instructions below. You can ask an adult for help.

Circle the country you live in.

Write the name of your country.

....

Write the name of the leader of your country.

....

What language do most people speak in your country?

....

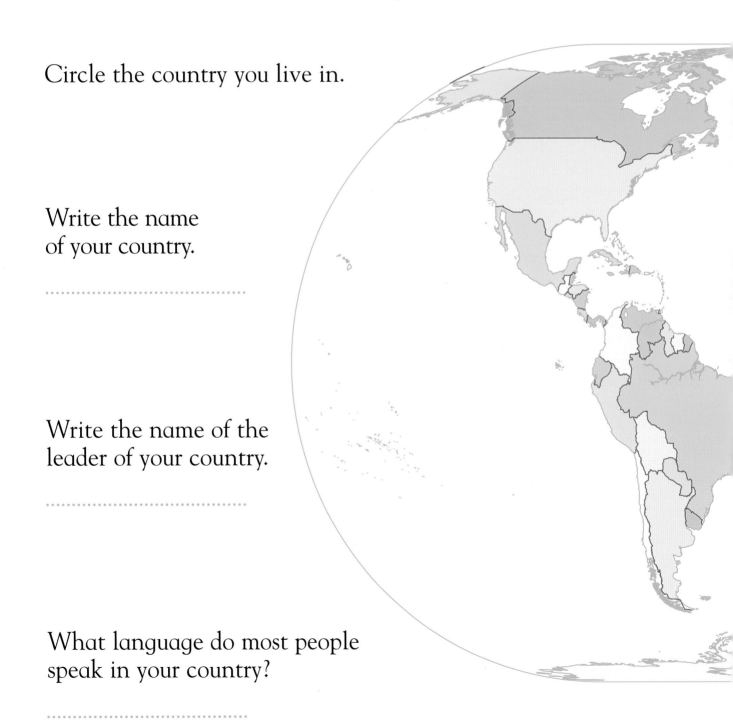

All the people in a country share the same leader, such as a president or a queen. They usually speak the same language. Every country has its own flag, too.

FACTS

Many countries are divided into smaller regions. In some countries, like the United States (US), these smaller regions are called states.

Here is a map of the United States, which is one large country.

If you live in the US, color in your state. If you don't live in the US, color in a state you would like to visit.

What is the name of the state you colored?

....

Name a state that is next to the state you colored.

....

Name a state that is far away from the state you colored.

....

The United States is divided into 50 states. A few of these states are small, but some are very large and are filled with many towns and cities.

FACTS

Some countries are divided into smaller regions known as provinces, rather than states. Canada has ten provinces (and three other regions called territories).

Look at the map of Canada above.

The name of one of the provinces begins with the letter **O**. Find this province and color it blue.

The name of one of the provinces begins with the letter **Q**. Find this province and color it green.

FACTS

A city is a busy place filled with people. There are many roads, houses, and buildings close together in a city. A big city may also have museums, parks, theaters, sports stadiums, and airports.

Look at this map showing a part of a city. Then follow the instructions given below.

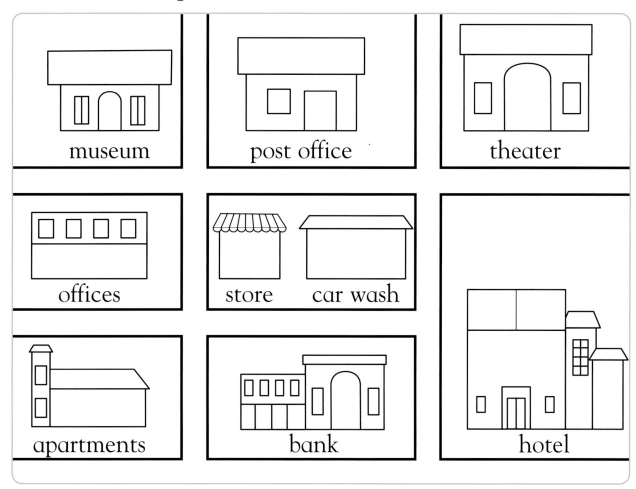

museum

post office

theater

offices

store   car wash

apartments

bank

hotel

Name three things in this city.

....

....

....

FACTS

Our Earth is a very big planet. The land on Earth is divided into seven large continents. These continents are further divided into countries.

Look at the shaded areas in each pair of globes below. Which is bigger? Circle the correct globe.

 planet Earth

 continent of North America

 continent of Australia

 continent of Asia

 continent of Africa

 country of Nigeria

Some countries are divided into states, as we learned on pages 30 and 31. Some states are very big, while others are very small. States have cities, which can be big or small.

Look at the shaded areas in each pair of maps below. Which is bigger? Circle the correct map.

United States of America

state of California

state of Texas

state of Ohio

Portland

city of Portland

OREGON

state of Oregon

FACTS

Maps tell us about a place using symbols, sometimes shown as pictures. The symbols are explained in what is known as a key. A map's key is a list of the different symbols that the map uses. It helps you read the map.

Match each map symbol to the thing you think it stands for. Ask a grown up for help.

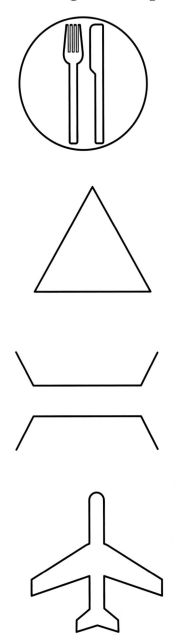

FACTS

It can be hard for people to find their way around the natural world without a map. Nature maps tell you what you will find in an area of the natural world. Each symbol in the key stands for a different part of the natural world.

Look at this nature map. Then follow the instructions given below.

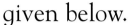

Draw lines to connect each symbol to the name of the place it stands for.

forest

lake

river

mountain

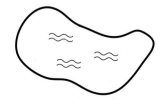

FACTS

A city is a big place. Maps can help you find your way around a city. They show you which roads you can take. A city map also shows you where to find the places you want. Without a map, it is easy to get lost.

Look at this map of a part of a city. Draw a line to connect each symbol on the map to the name of the place you think it stands for.

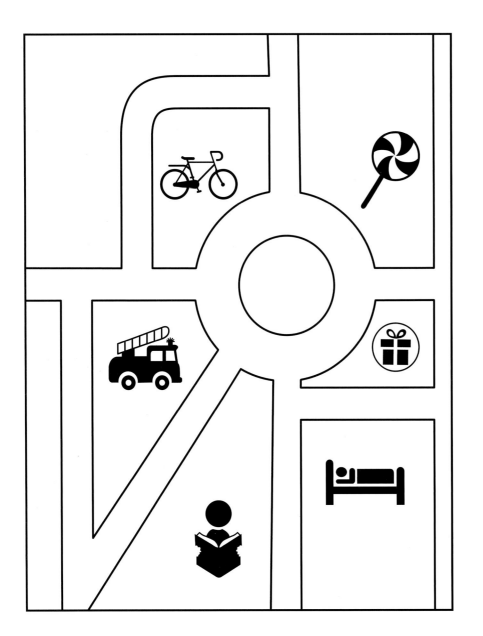

bike store

candy store

gift shop

hotel

fire department

library

A map of a park can show you the activities you can do there. It can also show you how to get to the places you want to visit. The map also shows you where to get help.

Look at the map of a park below. Then, read the list of activities you can do in the park. Draw a line to connect each activity to the symbol on the map that it stands for.

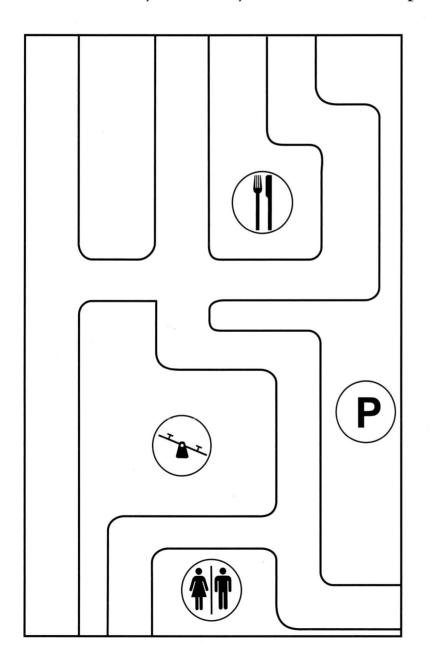

play on the see-saw

eat a picnic

use the restroom

park your car

FACTS

Some map keys use symbols that are not pictures. Instead, they use letters as symbols to tell you what to find there.

Look at this map of a school and its key. The key uses letters to represent different places in the school.

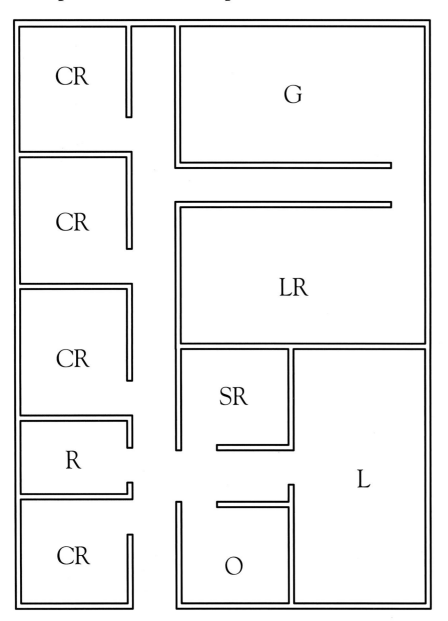

Key

LR	lunch room
O	office
SR	science room
L	library
G	gym
R	restroom
CR	classroom

Imagine you are at the gym and you need to reach the restroom. Draw a path on the map to find your way.

Some map keys do not use words at all. They have symbols that are small pictures of the places or things that are shown on the map.

Look at this map of a zoo. It has small pictures of animals as symbols to show where each can be found in the zoo.

Key

Imagine you are standing in front of the lions. You want to go see the alligators. Draw a path on the map to find your way.

FACTS

Road maps are some of the most commonly used maps. They can show you the roads in a town or a city, or roads that cross much larger areas, such as the highways running from state to state across the whole country.

Here is a map of three states in the US. The states are Washington, Oregon, and California. Use the compass rose to help you answer the questions below.

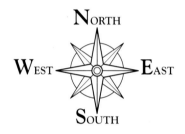

If you are in Oregon, in which direction would you drive to go up to Washington?

If you are in Oregon, in which direction would you drive to go down to California?

What is the route number of the road you would take to visit these places?

Key

5 interstate highway

A map of your neighborhood can help you find your way around the area close to your home. It can also show you the different kinds of places you will find there.

Imagine the map below is of your neighborhood. Answer the questions that follow, using the map, its key, and the compass rose.

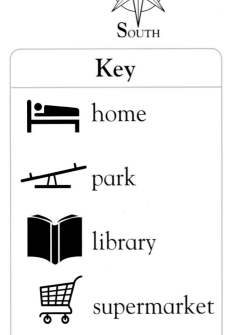

Which is closer to the park, the school or the supermarket?

....

What is to the east of your home?

....

If you are at the school, in which direction will you go to reach the library?

....

FACTS

Some maps tell you the choices you have when you visit a place. A park map, for example, helps you plan what you might do when you visit that park.

Look at this park map. Use direction words such as "left," "right," "next to," "in front of," and similar words to describe the path you would take to enjoy the activities given below. Trace your path on the map using your finger.

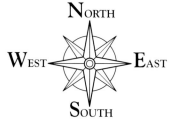

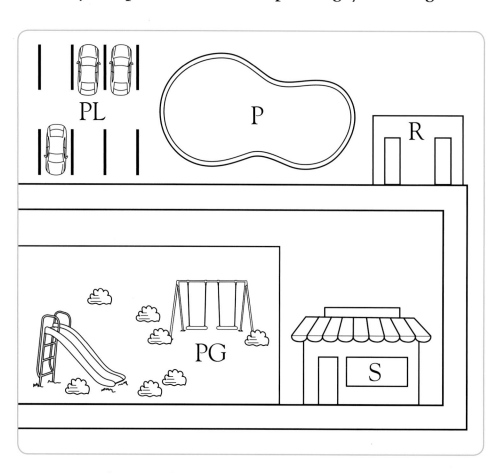

Key

PG	playground
PL	parking lot
R	restroom
S	snack bar
P	pool

Start at the parking lot. Then go to the pool. After swimming, wash your hands in the restroom. Then go down to the snack bar. After eating in the snack bar, play at the playground. That's a busy day at the park.
Where is the restroom? It is .... the pool.

A map can also help you to find your way when you are inside a building. You can still use a compass rose with this type of map.

Look at this map of a school. Answer the questions below, using only the map and the compass rose to help you.

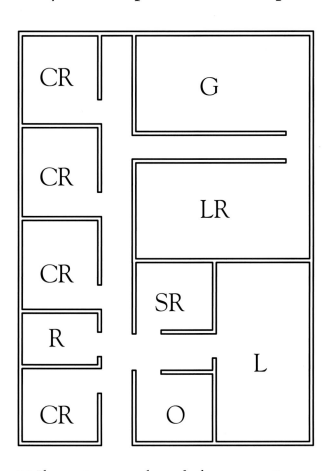

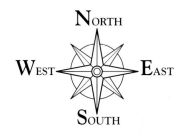

Key

LR	lunch room
O	office
SR	science room
L	library
G	gym
R	restroom
CR	classroom

What is south of the gym? ....

What is north of the lunch room? ....

What is to the east of the office? ....

Which rooms are on either side of the restroom? ....

Where do you want to go? What do you want to do? When you want to answer these questions, you use a map.

Jess and Miguel need different kinds of maps. Read about their trips below. Then put a check (✓) next to the map that each child needs.

Jess and her mother are driving across the United States to see Grandma and Grandpa.

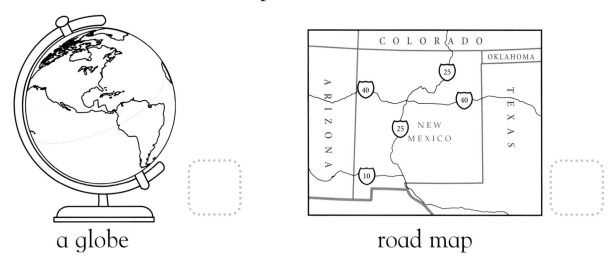

a globe   road map

Miguel and his brother are going to the video-game store in their town.

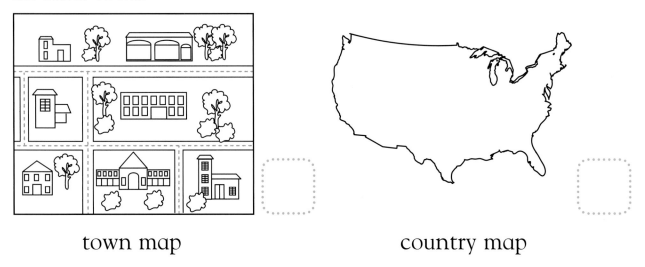

town map   country map

There are different kinds of maps. Each map is useful at a different time. Which map do you need?

Tanya and Leon also need maps. Below, read about what they need them for. Then put a check (✔) next to the map that each child needs.

Tanya and her parents are planning to buy furniture for their house.

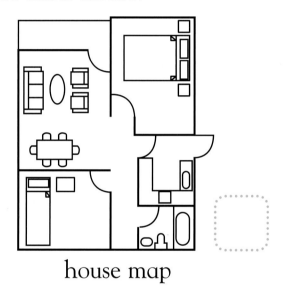

house map

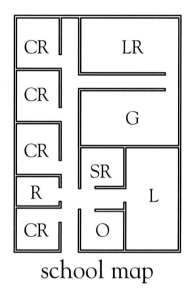

school map

Leon and his babysitter want to go for a picnic in a park.

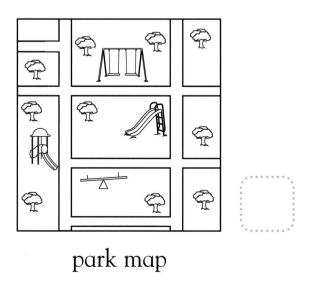

park map

a globe

Certificate

K

Congratulations to

....

for successfully finishing this book.

GOOD JOB!

You're a star.

Date

....

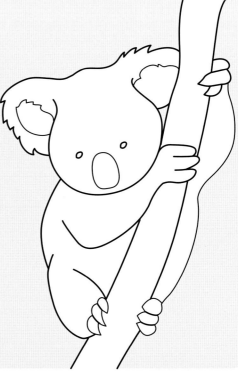

Answer Section
with Parents' Notes

This book is intended to support the geography concepts that are taught to your child in kindergarten. It includes activities that test your child's knowledge of the world around him or her. By working through this book, your child will be able to practice basic geography concepts in a fun and informative way.

Contents

These activities are intended to be completed by a child with adult support. The topics covered are as follows:

- Planet Earth and globes;
- The natural and the human (man-made) world;
- Bodies of water such as oceans, rivers, and lakes;
- Landforms such as mountains, hills, islands, and deserts;
- Types of maps and their keys;
- Compass directions;
- Continents, countries, provinces, and territories;
- Cities and states.

How to Help Your Child

As you work through the pages with your child, make sure he or she understands what each activity requires. Read the facts and instructions aloud. Encourage questions and reinforce observations that will build confidence and increase active participation in classes at school.

By working with your child, you will understand how he or she thinks and learns. When appropriate, use props and objects from daily life to help your child make connections with the world outside.

If an activity seems too challenging for your child, encourage him or her to try another page. You can also give encouragement by praising progress made as a correct answer is given and a page is completed.
Good luck, and remember to have fun!

Geography is about the world around you. The people who study geography are called geographers. Geographers study nature. They study things such as the mountains, rivers, and forests. Geographers also study the way humans use and change nature when they make things like cities, parks, and bridges.

Circle the things that a geographer might study.

mountain

city

butterfly

dinosaur

river

Ask your child why he or she thinks it might be interesting to learn about the world around them. Encourage your child to share with you questions or thoughts about the subject. This will spark an interest in geography.

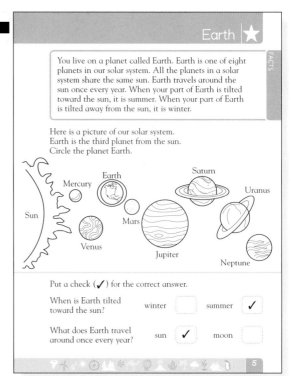

You live on a planet called Earth. Earth is one of eight planets in our solar system. All the planets in a solar system share the same sun. Earth travels around the sun once every year. When your part of Earth is tilted toward the sun, it is summer. When your part of Earth is tilted away from the sun, it is winter.

Here is a picture of our solar system. Earth is the third planet from the sun. Circle the planet Earth.

Sun   Mercury   Earth   Saturn   Uranus
Venus   Mars   Jupiter   Neptune

Put a check (✓) for the correct answer.

When is Earth tilted toward the sun?   winter ☐   summer ✓

What does Earth travel around once every year?   sun ✓   moon ☐

Explain that Earth is the only planet in our solar system people can live on. It is just the right distance from the sun to allow us to live at comfortable temperatures. Let your child point to planets that would be too hot and too cold for us.

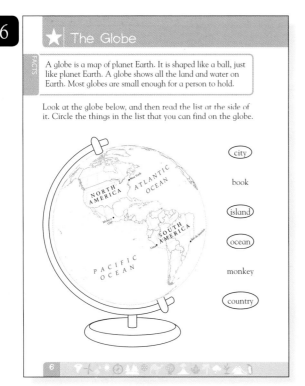

A globe is a map of planet Earth. It is shaped like a ball, just like planet Earth. A globe shows all the land and water on Earth. Most globes are small enough for a person to hold.

Look at the globe below, and then read the list at the side of it. Circle the things in the list that you can find on the globe.

NORTH AMERICA   ATLANTIC OCEAN   SOUTH AMERICA   PACIFIC OCEAN

city
book
island
ocean
monkey
country

If you have a globe at home, encourage your child to spend time exploring it. Ask your child to point out features on the globe that he or she notices. Point out where you live. If you do not have a globe at home, try your local library.

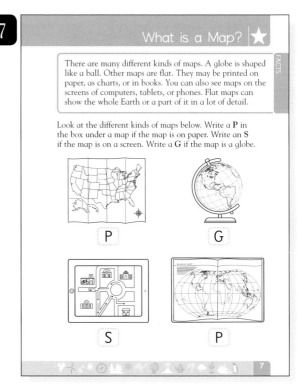

There are many different kinds of maps. A globe is shaped like a ball. Other maps are flat. They may be printed on paper, as charts, or in books. You can also see maps on the screens of computers, tablets, or phones. Flat maps can show the whole Earth or a part of it in a lot of detail.

Look at the different kinds of maps below. Write a **P** in the box under a map if the map is on paper. Write an **S** if the map is on a screen. Write a **G** if the map is a globe.

P   G
S   P

Conduct a treasure hunt at home to find maps! Find road maps, transit maps, travel books with maps, or maps on mobile devices. Help your child identify what each type of map shows, and how it is useful.

8

★ Types of Maps

Different maps are used to show and explain different kinds of places. A park map shows you what is in a park. A street map shows you the streets you can travel along. A map of a room shows you the things in that room.

Below are pictures of three different places: a city, a park, and a bedroom. Draw a line to connect each place with its map.

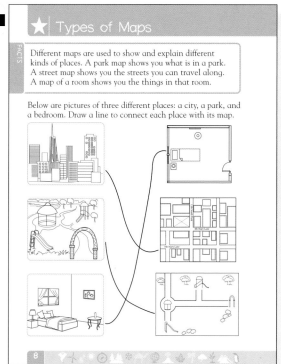

Encourage your child to use crayons or markers to draw a colorful map of his or her bedroom. Brainstorm the important features that should be included on the map. Mention that some maps are actually considered works of art!

9

Types of Maps ★

People use different maps for different reasons. A person driving a car may use a street map. Hikers may need a park map. Students and teachers may need a map of their school. There are many other kinds of maps as well.

Look at the different types of maps below. Who would use each kind of map? Draw a line to connect each map with the people who may need it.

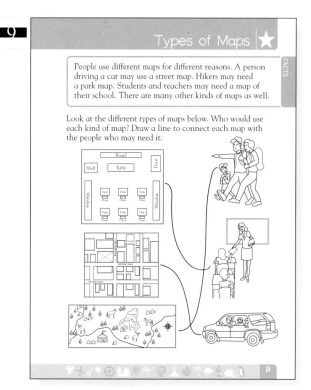

Tell your child how and when you use maps in your daily life. Give examples of common maps you use and their types—paper maps, electronic maps, or both. The next time you use a map, invite your child to read it with you.

10

★ Directions

There are four directions that you need to know about to be able to read a map. Those directions are "north," "south," "east," and "west." No matter where you are, these directions can help you reach the place that you want to go to.

Look at the globe of Earth below.
Then place your finger in the middle of Earth.
Move your finger north, up to the **N**.
Now, move your finger south, down to the **S**.

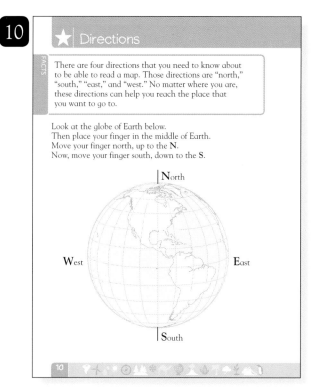

Explain to your child that since early times, people have used the sun and stars to find their way. Tell him or her that the sun rises in the east and sets in the west. Watch a sunrise or sunset to determine relative directions from your home.

Compass Rose ★

Most maps have a tool called a compass rose. It lets you know which direction the top of the map is pointing toward. Most maps have north at where the top and south at the bottom. On such maps, west is on the left and east is on the right.

This is the compass rose you will see on a map.
Color the compass rose. Trace in the letters **N**, **S**, **E**, and **W**.

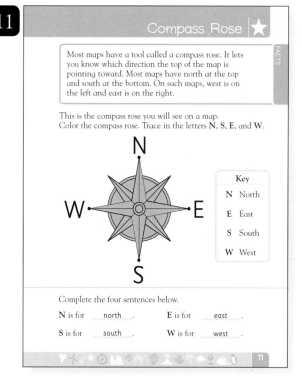

Key	
N	North
E	East
S	South
W	West

Complete the four sentences below.

N is for ___north___ . **E** is for ___east___ .

S is for ___south___ . **W** is for ___west___ .

Find a map that you commonly use and ask your child to point out the compass rose on the map. Encourage him or her to name the four directions on the rose.

★ North

The direction "north" is usually found at the top of a map. When you are going north, you are moving toward the top of Earth. You may know about the frozen North Pole. That is where you will end up if you keep going north!

Find the word "north" on the compass rose, and then circle it.

Now, look at the map of an amusement park below. Imagine you are standing at the X (✗). Which two rides are to the north of you? Circle them on the map.

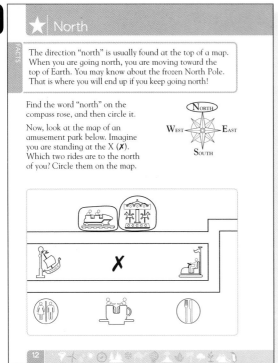

Determine where north is in relation to your home. Challenge your child to point out things and places that are north of your home.

13

South ★

The direction "south" is usually found at the bottom of a map. When you are going south, you are moving toward the bottom of Earth. Have you heard about the freezing South Pole? That is where you will find yourself if you keep going south!

Find the word "south" on the compass rose, and then circle it. Now look at the map of North America. Find the country of Canada. Then color the country directly south of Canada.

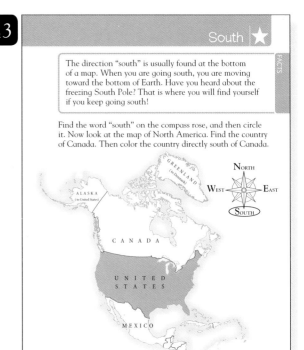

After having figured out which direction is north, stand in the center of the area where you are. Then ask your child to stand south of your position. Remind him or her that south is the opposite of north.

14

★ East

The direction "east" is usually found at the right side of a map. When you are going east, you are moving sideways across Earth from left to right. Did you know that the sun rises in the east?

Look at the town map below. Imagine you are standing at the X (✗). Which two buildings are to the east of you? Circle them on the map.

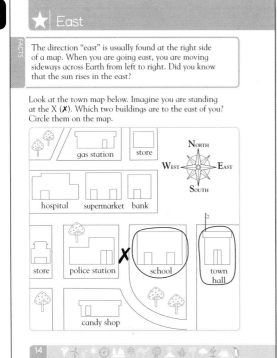

Find a map of your city or town. Find street names or areas that contain the word "East." Together, talk about why the street or area may be called "East."

15

West ★

The direction "west" is usually at the left side of a map. When you are going west, you are moving across Earth from right to left. The sun sets in the west. If you can see the sun setting, you are facing west, and it is time for bed!

Look at the map of Australia below. It shows where some animals are found. Imagine you are standing at the X (✗). Circle the animal that can be found to the west of you.

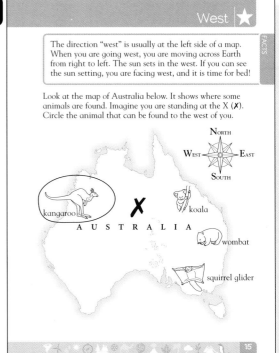

Having determined the four directions around your area, reinforce them by directing your child to walk north, south, east, and then west. Have fun with directions by making quick, silly turns!

★ The Natural World

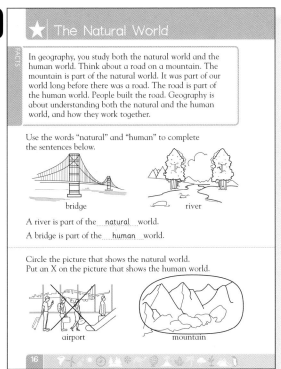

In geography, you study both the natural world and the human world. Think about a road on a mountain. The mountain is part of the natural world. It was part of our world long before there was a road. The road is part of the human world. People built the road. Geography is about understanding both the natural and the human world, and how they work together.

Use the words "natural" and "human" to complete the sentences below.

bridge   river

A river is part of the ___natural___ world.
A bridge is part of the ___human___ world.

Circle the picture that shows the natural world.
Put an X on the picture that shows the human world.

airport   mountain

Help your child make a collage of the natural world, using pictures found in magazines and newspapers. Selecting the pictures will help reinforce the concept of the natural world versus the human world.

Your World ★

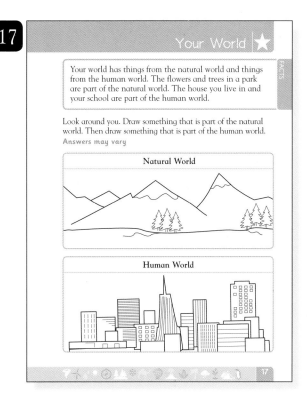

Your world has things from the natural world and things from the human world. The flowers and trees in a park are part of the natural world. The house you live in and your school are part of the human world.

Look around you. Draw something that is part of the natural world. Then draw something that is part of the human world.
Answers may vary

Natural World

Human World

As you travel around town with your child, encourage him or her to point out examples of the human world and the natural world. Then you can explain the ways in which the human world and the natural world work together.

★ Natural World Maps

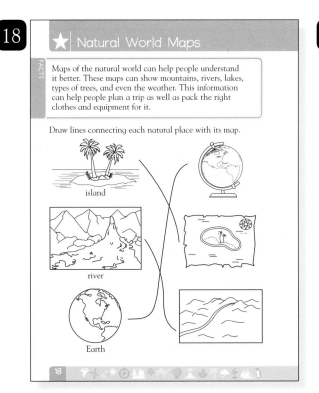

Maps of the natural world can help people understand it better. These maps can show mountains, rivers, lakes, types of trees, and even the weather. This information can help people plan a trip as well as pack the right clothes and equipment for it.

Draw lines connecting each natural place with its map.

island

river

Earth

Maps help people plan what they need for a trip, so they can dress for the weather or carry the right equipment for different conditions. Ask your child to imagine a visitor to your home today. What would your child suggest the visitor pack?

Continents ★

There are seven very large areas of land on Earth. These huge areas are called continents. When you look at a globe or a flat map of Earth, you will see the seven continents. The largest continent is Asia. The smallest continent is Australia.

Look at this map of the world. It shows all seven continents. Then follow the instructions below the map.

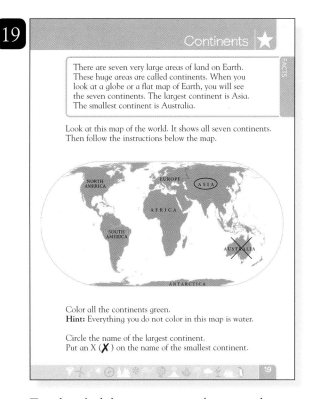

NORTH AMERICA EUROPE ASIA AFRICA SOUTH AMERICA AUSTRALIA ANTARCTICA

Color all the continents green.
Hint: Everything you do not color in this map is water.

Circle the name of the largest continent.
Put an X (✗) on the name of the smallest continent.

Together, find the continent you live on and point to it on the map. Explain to your child that no one lives permanently on the continent of Antarctica. Scientists work there, but they go home after a few weeks or months.

★ | Mountains and Hills

Mountains and hills are high areas of land. Hills are not as high as mountains. Some mountains are so tall that their tops reach the clouds. The tallest mountains have snow on top, even in summer.

Look at the two pictures below. Color the mountains brown. Color the hills green. Then answer the questions.

What is on top of the tallest mountain?   a flag

What is on top of the tallest hill?   a goat

Look up pictures of some famous mountains and mountain ranges, such as Mt. Everest or the Rocky Mountains, on the Internet. To point out the difference between mountains and hills, also look up hill ranges, such as the North Downs or South Downs in England.

Forests | ★

Forests are large areas of land that are covered with trees. There are many forests on Earth. Many different kinds of animals live inside a forest. Some are large and others are small.

Look at the picture of a forest below. There are many different kinds of animals living in this forest. Circle the animals that you can find.

Tell your child that forests are often shown in green on maps. Point out a forest on a map. If you live near a forest, take your child on a walk through it to experience it firsthand.

★ | Deserts

The driest places on Earth are called deserts. Many are very hot in the daytime and cold at night, but some are always cold. Deserts get very little rain. Most people do not like to live in such dry places. However, a number of plants and animals have learned to live in the desert.

Look at the picture of a desert below. Circle the different kinds of animals and plants that you can find in the picture.

With your child, explore more about how different animals and plants have adapted to live well in the dry desert. Look online or go to the library to find books about desert plants and animals.

Islands | ★

An island is a piece of land that is completely surrounded by water. Islands can be very large, or they can be very small.

Look at the islands of Hawaii below. Then complete the activities.

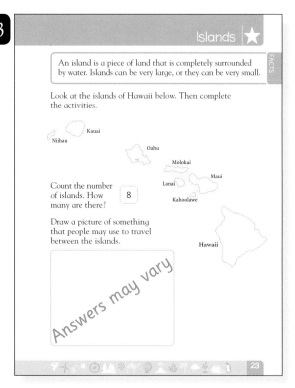

Kauai
Niihau
Oahu
Molokai
Lanai
Maui
Kahoolawe
Hawaii

Count the number of islands. How many are there?   8

Draw a picture of something that people may use to travel between the islands.

Answers may vary

Reinforce the idea that islands can be of different sizes. Greenland, in the Atlantic Ocean, is one of the world's largest islands. Nauru, in the Pacific Ocean, is the world's smallest island nation.

★ Oceans

FACTS

An ocean is a very, very large body of water. There are five oceans on Earth, and they cover most of the planet. They are home to many different kinds of animals, such as whales, sea turtles, and fish. In fact, there are more animals in the oceans than there are on land.

Look at the map of the world below. It shows the continents surrounded by oceans. Color the oceans.

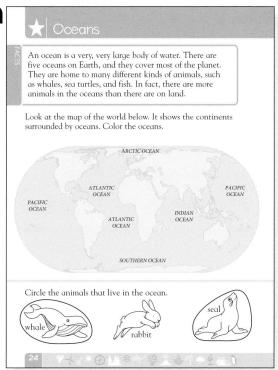

Circle the animals that live in the ocean.

whale   rabbit   seal

Ask your child if he or she can name the ocean that is closest to home. Look on a map together to check his or her answer or to find the answer.

Lakes ★

FACTS

A lake is a large body of water surrounded by land. Some lakes are very big. People would need a large boat to go across a big lake. Other lakes are much smaller. People can cross them in a small boat.

Circle the things made by humans that you might see at a lake. Color the animals that you might also see there.

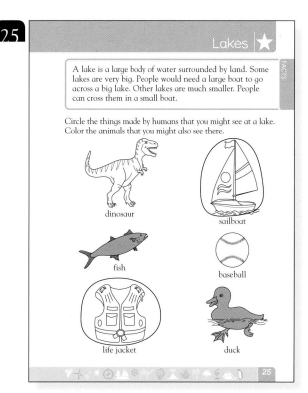

dinosaur   sailboat

fish   baseball

life jacket   duck

Are lakes part of the natural world or the human world? It depends on the lake! Explain to your child that some lakes are natural, and some were made by people.

★ Rivers

FACTS

Water flows from high places to low places. A small amount of flowing water is called a stream. A large amount of flowing water is called a river. Many towns and cities are built along rivers. Rivers can be long and wide and may move very quickly. You might need a bridge or a boat to get across a river.

Circle the three things you can use to get across a river.

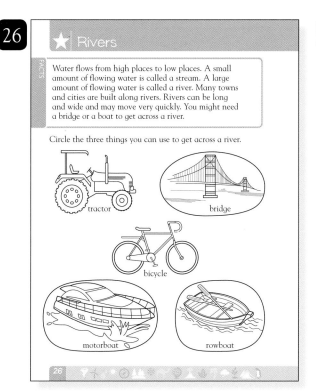

tractor   bridge

bicycle

motorboat   rowboat

Explain to your child that many animals, such as ducks, geese, otters, beavers, and alligators, make their homes in or near rivers. Rivers provide food and shelter that the animals need to live. Find out what animals live in or near rivers in your area.

The Human World ★

FACTS

The places humans make are part of the human world. We build roads, bridges, and tunnels to help us go places. We make cities, towns, and villages to live in. We create parks and playgrounds so we can enjoy them. All of these things can be found on a map.

Circle the pictures of things that belong to the human world.

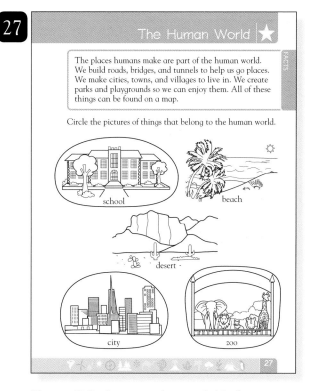

school   beach

desert

city   zoo

Play an "I Spy" game with your child where you take turns to guess whether the items you see around you are from the human world or the natural world. Start with "I spy something from the human world." That is the first clue!

★ | Countries

FACTS | A country is an area of Earth that people identify as one place.

Look at the map of the world. Then follow the instructions below. You can ask an adult for help.
Answers may vary

Circle the country you live in.

Write the name of your country.

....

Write the name of the leader of your country.

....

What language do most people speak in your country?

....

Talk to your child about what other countries people in your family have come from or lived in. Point them out on the map.

Countries | ★

FACTS | All the people in a country share the same leader, such as a president or a queen. They usually speak the same language. Every country has its own flag, too.

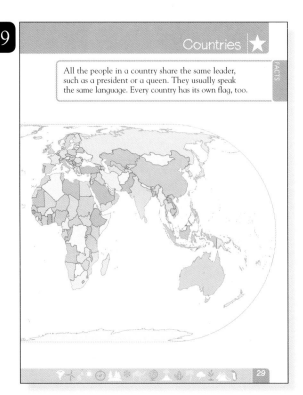

Your child might be curious to know how many countries there are in the world. There are about 200. If he or she is curious to learn more about another country, together find information about its geography, flag, language, and food.

★ | States

FACTS | Many countries are divided into smaller regions. In some countries, like the United States (US), these smaller regions are called states.

Here is a map of the United States, which is one large country.

If you live in the US, color in your state. If you don't live in the US, color in a state you would like to visit.
Answers may vary

What is the name of the state you colored?
Answers may vary

Name a state that is next to the state you colored.
Answers may vary

Name a state that is far away from the state you colored.
Answers may vary

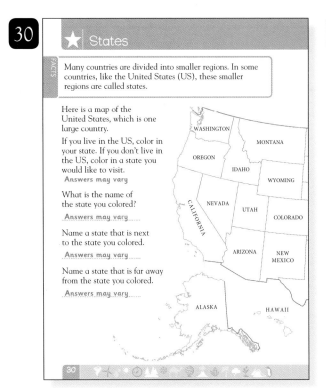

Point out states you have lived in or visited, or those you would like to visit. Count how many states you and your child have each been to. If you do not live in the United States, share facts that you know about any of the states.

States | ★

FACTS | The United States is divided into 50 states. A few of these states are small, but some are very large and are filled with many towns and cities.

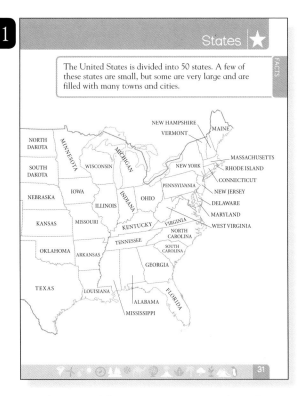

Use the map of the states to review and reinforce the four directions. Ask your child to point to the states in the north, east, south, and west. Let him or her find states that have a direction in their name, for example, North Carolina.

★ Provinces

Some countries are divided into smaller regions known as provinces, rather than states. Canada has ten provinces (and three other regions called territories).

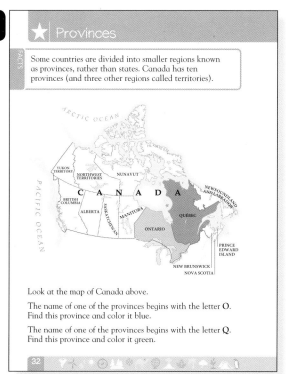

Look at the map of Canada above.

The name of one of the provinces begins with the letter **O**. Find this province and color it blue.

The name of one of the provinces begins with the letter **Q**. Find this province and color it green.

Some of the names of the provinces are long! Help your child learn the names of the provinces by pointing to each province and reading the name aloud to him or her.

Cities ★

A city is a busy place filled with people. There are many roads, houses, and buildings close together in a city. A big city may also have museums, parks, theaters, sports stadiums, and airports.

Look at this map showing a part of a city. Then follow the instructions given below.

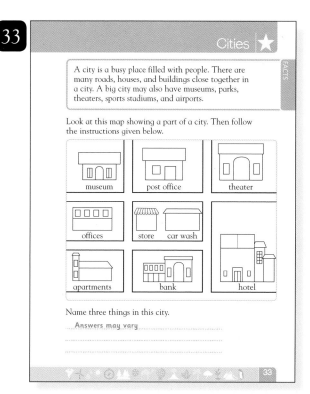

Name three things in this city.

Answers may vary

What is the biggest city near you? Or do you live in the biggest city in your area? Point out your city on a map. Then name the cities around you, pointing to each location, to help your child understand more about the geography of your area.

★ Which is Bigger?

Our Earth is a very big planet. The land on Earth is divided into seven large continents. These continents are further divided into countries.

Look at the shaded areas in each pair of globes below. Which is bigger? Circle the correct globe.

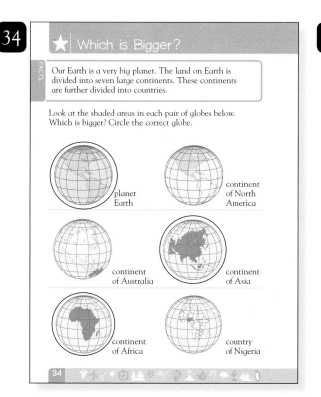

Extend the activity by having your child point out two sections on a globe or map and asking you which is bigger. He or she will gain confidence by being the "teacher" who knows the answer!

Which is Bigger? ★

Some countries are divided into states, as we learned on pages 30 and 31. Some states are very big, while others are very small. States have cities, which can be big or small.

Look at the shaded areas in each pair of maps below. Which is bigger? Circle the correct map.

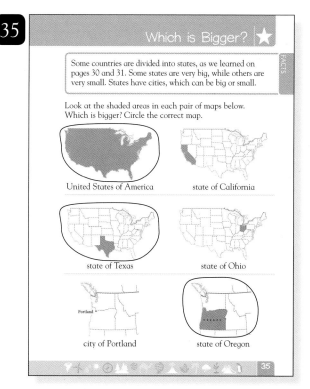

Look at the map of the United States together. Invite your child to find two states that are about the same size and shape.

★ Map Keys

Maps tell us about a place using symbols, sometimes shown as pictures. The symbols are explained in what is known as a key. A map's key is a list of the different symbols that the map uses. It helps you read the map.

Match each map symbol to the thing you think it stands for. Ask a grown up for help.

Reinforce the activity on map keys with a real-world example. Show your child maps that you have and ask him or her to point out their keys. Together, identify the different items on a key and find the symbols on the map.

Nature Map Key ★

It can be hard for people to find their way around the natural world without a map. Nature maps tell you what you will find in an area of the natural world. Each symbol in the key stands for a different part of the natural world.

Look at this nature map. Then follow the instructions given below.

Draw lines to connect each symbol to the name of the place it stands for.

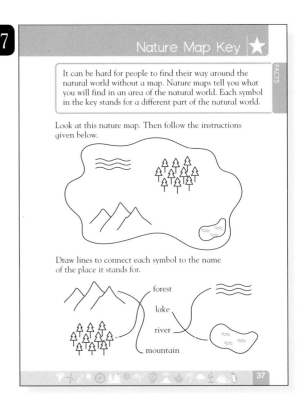

forest
lake
river
mountain

Invite your child to think of one more symbol to add to the nature map. Have him or her look around outside for ideas.

★ City Map Key

A city is a big place. Maps can help you find your way around a city. They show you which roads you can take. A city map also shows you where to find the places you want. Without a map, it is easy to get lost.

Look at this map of a part of a city. Draw a line to connect each symbol on the map to the name of the place you think it stands for.

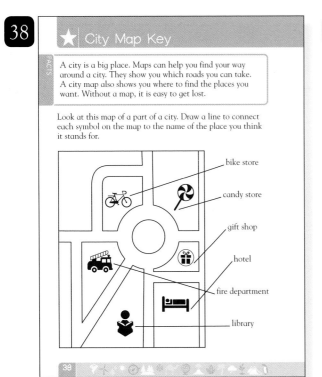

bike store
candy store
gift shop
hotel
fire department
library

Show your child a map of the city or town you live in. Point out important places that are known to your child: your home, school, friend's house, library, and so on. Which important place is closest to home? Which place is the farthest away?

Park Map Key ★

A map of a park can show you the activities you can do there. It can also show you how to get to the places you want to visit. The map also shows you where to get help.

Look at the map of a park below. Then, read the list of activities you can do in the park. Draw a line to connect each activity to the symbol on the map that it stands for.

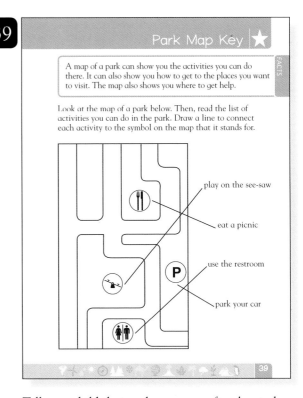

play on the see-saw
eat a picnic
use the restroom
park your car

Tell your child that park maps are often located at the entrance to a park, and in different spots around a park, depending on the park's size. Park maps can sometimes show the spot where the map reader is standing.

★ School Map Key

Some map keys use symbols that are not pictures. Instead, they use letters as symbols to tell you what to find there.

Look at this map of a school and its key. The key uses letters to represent different places in the school.

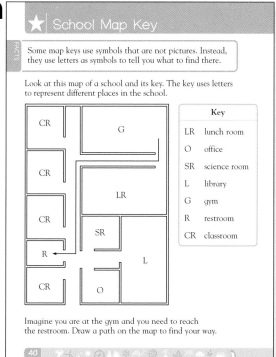

Key	
LR	lunch room
O	office
SR	science room
L	library
G	gym
R	restroom
CR	classroom

Imagine you are at the gym and you need to reach the restroom. Draw a path on the map to find your way.

Have your child think about his or her school. If you were to draw a map of the school, how would it be similar to or different from the school map shown on this page?

Zoo Map Key ★

Some map keys do not use words at all. They have symbols that are small pictures of the places or things that are shown on the map.

Look at this map of a zoo. It has small pictures of animals as symbols to show where each can be found in the zoo.

Imagine you are standing in front of the lions. You want to go see the alligators. Draw a path on the map to find your way.

Invite your child to create an imaginary zoo map on a separate piece of paper. He or she might create a zoo of fantastical creatures, or one filled entirely with his or her favorite animals. Have your child include a map key.

★ Using a Road Map

Road maps are some of the most commonly used maps. They can show you the roads in a town or a city, or roads that cross much larger areas, such as the highways running from state to state across the whole country.

Here is a map of three states in the US. The states are Washington, Oregon, and California. Use the compass rose to help you answer the questions below.

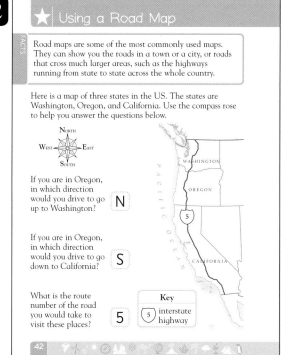

If you are in Oregon, in which direction would you drive to go up to Washington? **N**

If you are in Oregon, in which direction would you drive to go down to California? **S**

What is the route number of the road you would take to visit these places? **5**

Key	
⑤	interstate highway

Explain to your child that many highways in the US have numbers for names. Interstate highways that travel east and west use even numbers. Interstate highways that travel north and south have odd numbers.

Using a Neighborhood Map ★

A map of your neighborhood can help you find your way around the area close to your home. It can also show you the different kinds of places you will find there.

Imagine the map below is of your neighborhood. Answer the questions that follow, using the map, its key, and the compass rose.

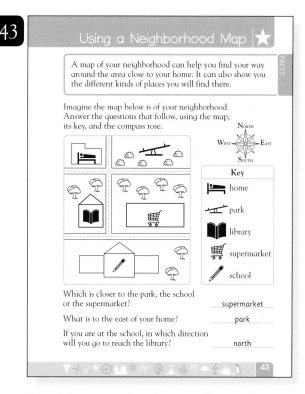

Key	
🛏	home
🛝	park
📖	library
🛒	supermarket
✏	school

Which is closer to the park, the school or the supermarket? supermarket

What is to the east of your home? park

If you are at the school, in which direction will you go to reach the library? north

Extend the activity by taking a walk around your neighborhood with your child. Take turns pointing out the things you would include if you were making a map of the neighborhood.

FACTS Some maps tell you the choices you have when you visit a place. A park map, for example, helps you plan what you might do when you visit that park.

Look at this park map. Use direction words such as "left," "right," "next to," "in front of," and similar words to describe the path you would take to enjoy the activities given below. Trace your path on the map using your finger.

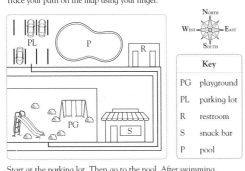

Key

PG	playground
PL	parking lot
R	restroom
S	snack bar
P	pool

Start at the parking lot. Then go to the pool. After swimming, wash your hands in the restroom. Then go down to the snack bar. After eating in the snack bar, play at the playground. That's a busy day at the park.
Where is the restroom? It is __next to/east of__ the pool.

Have your child practice giving directions to others. Ask him or her to give you directions from where you are to another room, such as a bathroom. Reinforce their use of direction words, such as left, right, and straight ahead.

FACTS A map can also help you to find your way when you are inside a building. You can still use a compass rose with this type of map.

Look at this map of a school. Answer the questions below, using only the map and the compass rose to help you.

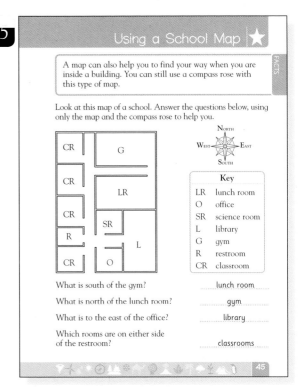

Key

LR	lunch room
O	office
SR	science room
L	library
G	gym
R	restroom
CR	classroom

What is south of the gym? __lunch room__

What is north of the lunch room? __gym__

What is to the east of the office? __library__

Which rooms are on either side of the restroom? __classrooms__

A museum is another type of building that might have a map. Go online to find maps for the museums that are near you or of interest to you and your child. Have your child describe what they see in each map.

FACTS Where do you want to go? What do you want to do? When you want to answer these questions, you use a map.

Jess and Miguel need different kinds of maps. Read about their trips below. Then put a check (✓) next to the map that each child needs.

Jess and her mother are driving across the United States to see Grandma and Grandpa.

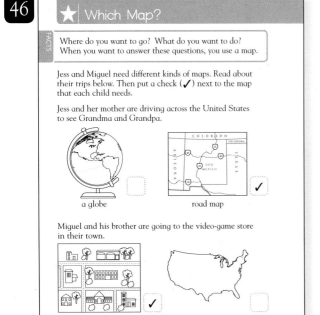

a globe   road map ✓

Miguel and his brother are going to the video-game store in their town.

town map ✓   country map

Ask your child to describe scenarios when someone might need the park map and the country map. Let your child take the lead and you can fill in details if necessary.

FACTS There are different kinds of maps. Each map is useful at a different time. Which map do you need?

Tanya and Leon also need maps. Below, read about what they need them for. Then put a check (✓) next to the map that each child needs.

Tanya and her parents are planning to buy furniture for their house.

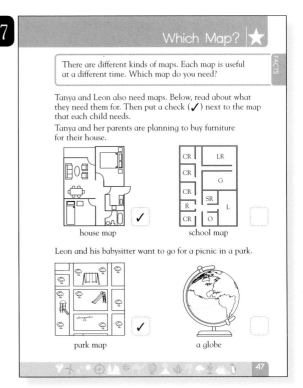

house map ✓   school map

Leon and his babysitter want to go for a picnic in a park.

park map ✓   a globe

Ask your child to describe scenarios when someone might need the school map and the globe. Let your child take the lead and you can fill in details if necessary.